The OCEAN
El OCÉANO

SECOND EDITION

By Sindy McKay

Translated by Yanitzia Canetti

TREASURE **BAY**

Family Engagement in Reading

Parent's Introduction

Whether your child is a beginning, reluctant, or eager reader, this book offers a fun and easy way to support your child in reading.

Developed with reading education specialists, We Both Read books invite you and your child to take turns reading aloud. You read the left-hand pages of the book, and your child reads the right-hand pages—which have been written at one of six early reading levels. The result is a wonderful new reading experience and faster reading development!

This is a special bilingual edition of a We Both Read book. On each page the text is in two languages. This offers the opportunity for you and your child to read in either language. It also offers the opportunity to learn new words in another language.

In some books, a few challenging words are introduced in the parent's text with **bold** lettering. Pointing out and discussing these words can help to build your child's reading vocabulary. If your child is a beginning reader, it may be helpful to run a finger under the text as each of you reads. Please also notice that a "talking parent" icon ⊚ precedes the parent's text, and a "talking child" icon ⊚ precedes the child's text.

If your child struggles with a word, you can encourage "sounding it out," but not all words can be sounded out. Your child might pick up clues about a difficult word from other words in the sentence or a picture on the page. If your child struggles with a word for more than five seconds, it is usually best to simply say the word.

As you read together, praise your child's efforts and keep the reading fun. Simply sharing the enjoyment of reading together will increase your child's skills and help to start your child on a lifetime of reading enjoyment!

Introducción a los padres

Ya sea que su hijo sea un lector principiante, reacio o ansioso, este libro ofrece una manera fácil y divertida de ayudarlo en la lectura.

Desarrollado con especialistas en educación de lectura, los libros We Both Read lo invita a usted y a su hijo a turnarse para leer en voz alta. Usted lee las páginas de la izquierda del libro y su hijo lee las páginas de la derecha, que se han escrito en uno de seis primeros niveles de lectura. ¡El resultado es una nueva y maravillosa experiencia de lectura y un desarrollo más rápido de la misma!

Esta es una edición especial bilingüe de un libro de We Both Read. En cada página el texto aparece en dos idiomas. Esto le ofrece la oportunidad de que usted y su hijo lean en cualquiera de los dos idiomas. También le ofrece la oportunidad de aprender nuevas palabras en otro idioma.

En algunos libros, se presentan en el texto de los padres algunas palabras difíciles con letras **en negrita.** Señalar y discutir estas palabras puede ayudar a desarrollar el vocabulario de lectura de su hijo. Si su hijo es un lector principiante, puede ser útil deslizar un dedo debajo del texto a medida que cada uno de ustedes lea. Tenga en cuenta también que un ícono de "padre que habla" precede al texto del padre y que un ícono de "niño que habla" precede al texto del niño.

Si su hijo tiene dificultad con una palabra, puede animarlo a "pronunciarla", pero no todas las palabras se pueden pronunciar fácilmente. Su hijo puede obtener pistas sobre una palabra difícil a partir de otras palabras en la oración o de una imagen en la página. Si su hijo tiene dificultades con una palabra durante más de cinco segundos, por lo general es mejor decir simplemente la palabra.

Mientras leen juntos, elogie los esfuerzos de su hijo y mantenga la diversión de la lectura. ¡El simple hecho de compartir el placer de leer juntos aumentará las destrezas de su hijo y lo ayudará a que disfrute de la lectura para toda la vida!

The Ocean • *El océano*

Second Edition

A We Both Read Book • *Un libro de la serie We Both Read*
Level 1-2 • *Niveles 1–2*
Guided Reading: Level H • *Lectura guiada: Nivel H*

With special thanks to
Rebecca Albright, Ph.D.,
Curator, California Academy of Sciences,
for her advice on the material in this book

*Con especial agradecimiento a
Rebecca Albright, Ph.D.,
Curadora, Academia de Ciencias de California,
por sus consejos sobre el material de este libro*

To Bonnie and Jeremy —and all who come after them
A Bonnie y Jeremy, y a todos los que vienen tras ellos
— S. M.

Use of photographs provided by iStock, Dreamstime, PhotoDisc, and Corbis Images.

We Both Read® is a registered trademark of Treasure Bay, Inc.

Published by Treasure Bay, Inc.
P.O. Box 119
Novato, CA 94948 USA

Printed in Malaysia

Library of Congress Catalog Card Number: 2016945521

ISBN: 978-1-60115-082-0

Visit us online at WeBothRead.com

PR-11-19

TABLE OF CONTENTS
CONTENIDO

Imagine you are a space alien flying high above **Earth**. You look down at the beautiful planet below, and what do you see? Water! You see lots and lots of water. Most of that water is contained in the **oceans** and seas of **Earth.**

*Imagina que eres un extraterrestre que vuela por encima de la **Tierra**. Miras hacia el hermoso planeta que hay abajo, ¿y qué ves? ¡Agua! Ves mucha, mucha agua. La mayor parte de esa agua está contenida en los **océanos** y mares de la **Tierra**.*

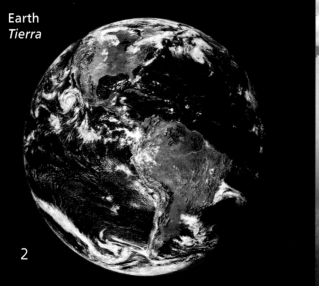

Earth
Tierra

2

Earth is covered by much more water than land. You could fit all the land on Earth into the **oceans** more than two times!

*La **Tierra** está cubierta por mucha más agua que tierra. ¡Toda la parte terrestre del planeta cabe más de dos veces en los **océanos**!*

3

Map of Earth
Mapa de la Tierra

North America
América del Norte

Atlantic Ocean
Océano Atlántico

Pacific Ocean
Océano Pacífico

South America
América del Sur

Southern Ocean
Océano Antártico

There are five major oceans on Earth: the **Pacific**, Atlantic, Indian, **Southern**, and Arctic. There are also many smaller seas. These oceans and most seas are all really one vast worldwide ocean that is broken up by big pieces of land we call continents.

*Hay cinco océanos principales en la Tierra: **Pacífico**, Atlántico, Índico, **Antártico** y Ártico. También hay muchos mares más pequeños. Estos océanos y la mayoría de los mares son realmente un vasto océano mundial que está dividido por grandes trozos de tierra que llamamos continentes.*

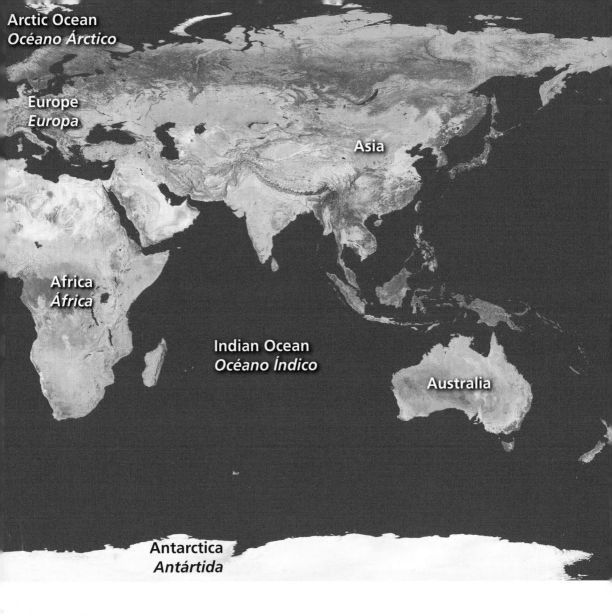

Arctic Ocean
Océano Ártico

Europe
Europa

Asia

Africa
África

Indian Ocean
Océano Índico

Australia

Antarctica
Antártida

The **Pacific** is the biggest ocean. You can sail on it for many days and never see land. The **Southern** Ocean is the part of the world's ocean that is closest to the South Pole.

*El **Pacífico** es el océano más grande. Puedes navegar en él por muchos días y nunca ver tierra. El Océano **Antártico** es la parte del océano del mundo más cerca del Polo Sur.*

When we look out at the sea, we see a vast expanse of water. But when we look under the ocean's surface, we find an amazing world filled with deep trenches, high mountains, dark caves, and colorful coral reefs. We also find an enormous variety of plants and animals from the tiny krill to the mighty whale.

Cuando miramos hacia el mar, vemos una vasta extensión de agua. Pero cuando miramos debajo de la superficie del océano, encontramos un mundo increíble lleno de trincheras profundas, altas montañas, cuevas oscuras y coloridos arrecifes de coral. También encontramos una enorme variedad de plantas y animales, desde el pequeño kril hasta la poderosa ballena.

Underwater cave
Cueva submarina

Longsnout seahorse
Caballito de mar mediterráneo

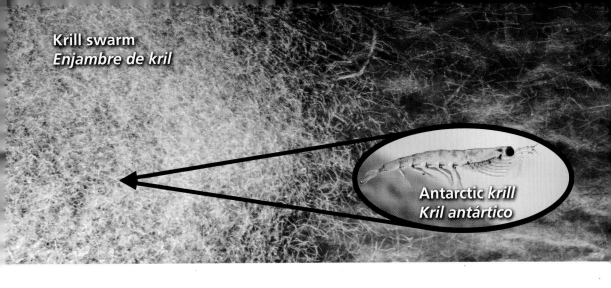

Krill swarm
Enjambre de kril

Antarctic *krill*
Kril antártico

There are very small animals in the ocean. Some are so small you can't even see them. There are also very big animals. Whales are some of the biggest animals to ever live on Earth.

Hay animales muy pequeños en el océano. Algunos son tan pequeños que ni puedes verlos. Hay también animales muy grandes. Las ballenas son algunos de los animales más grandes que jamás hayan vivido en la Tierra.

Humpback whale
Ballena jorobada

7

Algae floating in the ocean
Algas flotando en el océano

Protozoa plankton
(seen though a microscope)
Plancton protozoo
(visto a través de un microscopio)

Life in the ocean can be divided into three major groups. The first group, called **plankton**, includes the plants and animals that move and drift with the currents and tides. Some types of algae (AL-jee) are **plankton** that drift in the ocean. Other types of algae cling to the bottom of shallow waters, like tide pools. Some types of **plankton** can be large, like jellyfish with their long tentacles. However, most types of **plankton** are very tiny.

*La vida en el océano se puede dividir en tres grupos principales. El primer grupo, llamado **plancton**, incluye las plantas y los animales que se mueven y desplazan con las corrientes y las mareas. Algunos tipos de algas son **plancton** que flotan en el océano. Otros tipos de algas se adhieren al fondo de aguas poco profundas, como las pozas de marea. Algunos tipos de **plancton** pueden ser grandes, como las medusas con sus largos tentáculos. Sin embargo, la mayoría de los tipos de **plancton** son muy pequeños.*

Tide pool
Poza de marea

Green algae
Algas verdes

Pacific sea nettle jellyfish
Ortiga de mar del Pacífico

These tentacles
have stinging venom.

*Estos tentáculos tienen
un veneno punzante.*

Most animal **plankton** are not very strong. They drift as the movement of the water pushes them. That is mainly how they move around the oceans.

*La mayoría del **plancton** animal no es muy fuerte. Se desplazan a medida que el movimiento del agua los empuja. Así es principalmente como se mueven a través de los océanos.*

Stove pipe sponge
Esponja tubular

Stylophora coral
Coral Stylophora

Red sea anemone
Anémona marina roja

Sea fan
Abanico de mar

A second group of plants and animals that live in the ocean, called the benthos, live in the ocean floor. This group contains such unique life forms as coral, sponges, anemones (uh-NEM-uh-nees), sea stars, crabs, clams, and **sea** squirts. Corals and sponges are animals, but they do not have brains or **eyes**.

*Un segundo grupo de plantas y animales que viven en el océano, llamados bentos, viven en el fondo del océano. Este grupo contiene formas de vida únicas, como corales, esponjas, anémonas, estrellas de **mar**, cangrejos, almejas y ascidias. Los corales y las esponjas son animales, pero no tienen cerebro ni **ojos**.*

This is a **sea** star. It is a sea animal, but it is not a fish. Most sea stars have one tiny **eye** on the tip of each arm.

*Esta es una estrella de **mar**. Es un animal marino, pero no es un pez. La mayoría de las estrellas de mar tienen un pequeño **ojo** en la punta de cada brazo.*

Giant clam
Almeja gigante

The giant clam seen in this picture has a body made up of two shells connected by large, strong muscles. That's why it's so hard to open a clamshell! A giant clam can weigh more than a gorilla and can live longer than people can.

La almeja gigante que se ve en esta imagen tiene un cuerpo formado por dos conchas conectadas por músculos grandes y fuertes. ¡Por eso es tan difícil abrir el caparazón! Una almeja gigante puede pesar más que un gorila y puede vivir más tiempo que la gente.

Sally lightfoot crabs
Abuetes negros o zayapas

Pygmy seahorse in a sea fan
Caballito de mar pigmeo en un abanico de mar

This is a sea fan. It looks like a plant, but it is an animal. There is a sea horse hiding in the sea fan. The sea horse looks a lot like the sea fan.

Este es un abanico de mar. Parece una planta, pero es un animal. Hay un caballito de mar escondido en el abanico de mar. El caballito de mar se parece mucho al abanico de mar.

The third major group of animals in the ocean is called nekton. These creatures swim freely through the water and include some of the most familiar of all sea life. A few of the creatures that belong in this group are whales, sharks, manta rays, sea turtles, and well over 20,000 different species of fish.

El tercer grupo importante de animales del océano se llama necton. Estas criaturas nadan libremente en el agua e incluyen a algunas de las especies más conocidas del mundo marino. Las ballenas, los tiburones, las mantas rayas, las tortugas marinas y más de 20 000 especies diferentes de peces pertenecen a este grupo.

Manta ray
Manta raya

Whale shark
Tiburón ballena

Cobia fish
Pez cobia

There are many different kinds of sharks. The biggest is called the whale shark. It is the biggest fish in the ocean. It may be big, but it eats only tiny plankton.

Hay muchos tipos diferentes de tiburones. El más grande se llama tiburón ballena. Es el pez más grande del océano. Puede ser grande, pero solo come plancton pequeño.

Whale shark
Tiburón ballena

15

Powder blue tang
Cirujano azul cielo

Some kinds of fish swim together in large groups called **schools**. These **schools** are usually made up of fish that are eaten as **prey** by larger fish. Maybe there really is safety in numbers!

*Algunos tipos de peces nadan juntos en grandes grupos llamados **cardúmenes**. Estos **cardúmenes** generalmente están compuestos de peces que son devorados al ser **presas** de peces más grandes. ¡Están tal vez a salvo en cantidades!*

Pygmy sweepers
Barredores pigmeos

Great white shark
Gran tiburón blanco

Dorsal fin
Aleta dorsal

Tail fin
Aleta de la cola

Pectoral fin
Aleta pectoral

Not all fish swim in **schools**. Some fish swim alone and hunt for other fish to eat. They often hunt at dusk, when it is hard for their **prey** to see them.

*No todos los peces nadan en **cardúmenes**. Algunos peces nadan solos y cazan otros peces para comer. Suelen cazar al atardecer, cuando es difícil que sus **presas** los vean.*

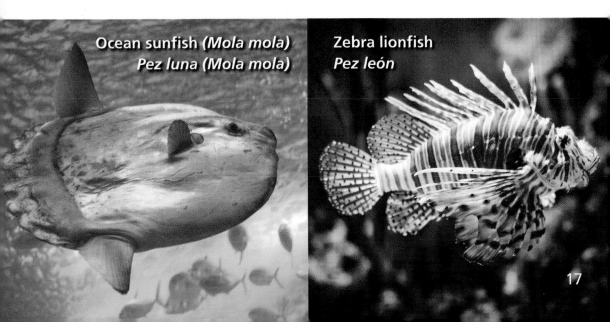

Ocean sunfish *(Mola mola)*
Pez luna (Mola mola)

Zebra lionfish
Pez león

Orca
Orca

Most of the animals in the ocean are able to breathe underwater. However, some ocean animals need to come to the surface to breathe. Whales, porpoises, and dolphins are mammals, just like us, and they would drown if they could not get to the surface for air.

La mayoría de los animales del océano son capaces de respirar bajo el agua. Sin embargo, algunos necesitan salir a la superficie para respirar. Las ballenas, las marsopas y los delfines son mamíferos, al igual que nosotros, y se ahogarían si no pudieran salir a la superficie a tomar aire.

Narwhal whales
Ballenas narvales

Tusk
Colmillo

Beluga whale
Ballena beluga

Bottlenose dolphins
Delfines nariz de botella

Dolphins like to be with other dolphins. They hunt and play together. They can see and hear very well, but they cannot smell.

A los delfines les gusta estar con otros delfines. Cazan y juegan juntos. Pueden ver y oír muy bien, pero no pueden oler.

Walrus
Morsa

Tusk
Colmillo

Sea lions, walruses, sea otters, and seals are mammals that spend much of their lives in the ocean. They might move slowly and clumsily on land, but they are swift and graceful in the water.

Los leones marinos, las morsas, nutrias marinas y focas son mamíferos que pasan la gran parte de su vida en el océano. Es posible que se muevan lentamente y torpemente en tierra, pero son rápidos y elegantes en el agua.

Sea lions
Leones marinos

Sea otter
Nutria marina

Most sea otters sleep on their backs in the water. All sea otters eat on their backs in the water. They like to eat fish, crabs, snails, and clams.

La mayoría de las nutrias marinas duermen boca arriba en el agua. Todas las nutrias marinas comen boca arriba en el agua. Les gusta comer pescado, cangrejos, caracoles y almejas.

Sea otter
Nutria marina

Green sea turtles
Tortugas marinas verdes

Sea turtle eggs
Huevos de tortugas marinas

Sea turtle hatchling
Cría de tortugas marinas

Sea turtles spend most of their time underwater, only coming to the surface to breathe. Female turtles must leave the water and come ashore to **build** nests and lay their eggs. Then they quickly return to the water, leaving the eggs to hatch on their own.

*Las tortugas marinas pasan la mayor parte del tiempo bajo el agua, y solo salen a la superficie para respirar. Las tortugas hembras deben abandonar el agua y bajar a tierra para **construir** nidos y poner sus huevos. Luego regresan rápidamente al agua, dejando que los huevos se incuben solos.*

Sea turtles **build** nests under the sand. After breaking out of its egg, a baby sea turtle must dig out of the sand. Then it must find its way to the ocean.

*Las tortugas marinas **construyen** nidos bajo la arena. Después de salir de su huevo, la tortuguita marina debe cavar para salir de la arena. Luego debe encontrar su camino hacia el océano.*

Brown pelican
Pelícano marrón

Sea birds fly in the air above the ocean and feed on plants and animals from the ocean. They come in many different shapes and sizes. One of the most unusual birds is the **penguin**.

*Las aves marinas vuelan sobre el océano y se alimentan de plantas y animales del océano. Tienen diferentes formas y tamaños. Una de las aves más inusuales es el **pingüino**.*

Sea gull
Gaviota

Blue-footed booby
Piquero de patas azules

24

Gentoo penguins
Pingüinos juanito

Penguins do not fly like most birds. They use their wings to help them swim. Some people say that they fly under the water!

*Los **pingüinos** no vuelan como la mayoría de las aves. Usan sus alas para nadar. ¡Algunas personas dicen que vuelan bajo el agua!*

Positano, Italy
Positano, Italia

Living in a city close to the ocean is important for many people, but the ocean is also important for everyone in the world. Most of the oxygen we breathe comes from the algae and plant plankton that grow in the ocean.

Vivir en una ciudad cercana al océano es importante para muchas personas, pero el océano también es importante para todos en el mundo. La mayor parte del oxígeno que respiramos proviene de las algas y el plancton vegetal que crecen en el océano.

San Francisco, California, USA.
San Francisco, California, EE. UU.

The ocean supports us in many ways. We get food from the ocean. Ships on the ocean can get us from place to place. We can even have fun at the beach!

El océano nos ayuda de muchas maneras. Obtenemos alimentos del océano. Los barcos nos pueden llevar de un lugar a otro en el océano. ¡Y hasta podemos divertirnos en la playa!

Boy swimming with green sea turtle
Niño nadando con una tortuga marina verde

People can have fun at an ocean beach. There they can swim, surf, snorkel, collect **seashells**, or just sit and listen to the **roar** of the waves. Once you have visited the ocean, you will want to return again and again!

*La gente puede divertirse en una playa del océano. Allí pueden nadar, hacer surf, bucear, recolectar **conchas marinas** o simplemente sentarse y escuchar el **rugido** de las olas. Una vez que hayas visitado el océano, ¡querrás volver una y otra vez!*

At some time in the past, each **seashell** on the beach was part of a live sea animal. Some **seashells** are very small and some are very big. If you hold a big **seashell** to your ear, you might hear a sound like the soft **roar** of the ocean.

*En algún momento del pasado, cada **concha** de la playa fue parte de un animal marino vivo. Algunas **conchas** son muy pequeñas y otras son muy grandes. Si colocas una **concha** grande en tu oreja, es posible que escuches un sonido como el suave **rugido** del océano.*

Snorkel
Tubo respirador

Mask
Máscara

Snorkeling is a great way to see what's going on underwater. It's wonderful to discover such an amazing world lying just beneath the ocean's surface.

Bucear es una excelente manera de ver lo que sucede bajo el agua. Es maravilloso descubrir un mundo tan asombroso como el que hay justo debajo del océano.

Fishing net
Red de pescar

Many people fish to get food. Some people do it just because they like to. It's a nice way to spend time with friends and family.

Mucha gente pesca para conseguir alimento. Algunas personas lo hacen solo porque les gusta. Es una buena manera de pasar tiempo con amigos y familiares.

Fishing pole
Caña de pescar

Kelp seaweed forest
Bosque de algas marinas

When most people think of the food that comes from the ocean, they think of fish. But there are many other kinds of food we harvest from the sea. In some countries, **seaweed** is used to make all kinds of delicious dishes!

*Cuando la mayoría de la gente piensa en la comida que proviene del océano, piensa en el pescado. Pero hay muchos otros tipos de alimentos que cosechamos del mar. En algunos países, ¡las **algas marinas** se utilizan para elaborar todo tipo de platos deliciosos!*

Do you eat ice cream? Then you may have eaten seaweed. One kind of **seaweed** is often used to make ice cream thick.

*¿Tomas helado? Entonces puede que hayas comido algas. Un tipo de **alga marina** se utiliza a menudo para hacer espeso el helado.*

Dried seaweed sheets (nori)
Hojas de algas marinas secas (nori)

Seaweed salad
Ensalada de algas marinas

Moving people and things across the vast ocean can be a real challenge. So people have built ships and boats of every size, from huge **freighters** to sleek sailboats to fancy cruise ships.

*Mover personas y cosas a través del vasto océano puede ser un verdadero desafío. Así que la gente ha construido barcos y embarcaciones de todos los tamaños, desde enormes **cargueros** y elegantes veleros hasta lujosos cruceros.*

Container ship going under the Golden Gate Bridge
Barco de contenedores pasando debajo el puente Golden Gate

Freighters are big ships that move cargo from one place to another place. They can carry cars, food, toys, and even airplanes.

*Los **cargueros** son grandes barcos que mueven la carga de un lugar a otro. Pueden transportar automóviles, alimentos, juguetes e incluso aviones.*

Scuba diver at shipwreck
Buzo en un barco hundido

Long ago big sailing ships would set out to **cruise** across the ocean. Occasionally one would end up sinking to the bottom of the sea. These old sunken ships can be found in places all across the oceans of the world. Some people try to find treasure in sunken ships. Do you think this one has any treasures on board?

*Hace mucho tiempo, los grandes barcos de vela zarpaban para **cruzar** el océano. Ocasionalmente alguno terminaría hundiéndose en el fondo del mar. Estos viejos barcos hundidos se pueden encontrar en todos los lugares del mundo a través de los océanos. Algunas personas tratan de encontrar tesoros en barcos hundidos. ¿Crees que este tiene algún tesoro a bordo?*

These days, **cruise** ships carry people across the ocean. Some of these ships are like small towns. They have places to eat, shop, sleep, and just have fun.

*En estos días, los **cruceros** llevan a la gente a través del océano. Algunos de estos barcos son como pequeñas ciudades. Tienen lugares para comer, comprar, dormir y divertirse.*

Unfortunately, one other way that humans use the ocean is as a dumping ground. Everything from trash to sewage to toxic waste goes into the sea. We used to think that the ocean could handle all that pollution, but now we know it can't.

Desafortunadamente, otra forma en que los humanos usan el océano es como vertedero. Todo, desde la basura hasta las aguas residuales y los desechos tóxicos, se introduce en el mar. Solíamos pensar que el océano podía manejar toda esa contaminación, pero ahora sabemos que no puede.

Big wave crashing
Gran ola rompiendo

You can help. You can find out more about the ocean. You can share all you know with other people.

Puedes ayudar. Puedes averiguar más sobre el océano. Puedes compartir todo lo que sabes con otras personas.

Picking up trash
Recogiendo basura

39

The more you know about the ocean, the more you appreciate how important it is. It is one of our most precious resources. Life on Earth could not exist without it.

Cuanto más sepas sobre el océano, más apreciarás lo importante que es. Es uno de nuestros recursos más preciados. La vida en la Tierra no podría existir sin este.

If we help take care of the ocean, the ocean will help take care of us.

Si ayudamos a cuidar el océano, el océano nos ayudará a cuidar de nosotros mismos.

Glossary • *Glosario*

continent • *continente*
one of the main landmasses on Earth • *una de las principales masas terrestres del planeta*

mammal • *mamífero*
an animal that breathes air and has at least some hair or fur on its body • *animal que respira aire y tiene algo de pelo en el cuerpo*

pollution • *contaminación*
harmful substances in the air or water • *sustancias nocivas en el aire o el agua*

predator • *depredador*
a fish or animal that hunts and eats other fish or animals • *un pez o animal que caza y come otros peces o animales*

school • *cardúmen*
a group of fish swimming together • *grupo de peces que nadan juntos*

tide pool • *pozo de marea*
a pool of water that remains after the tide goes out • *charco de agua que permanece después de que baja la marea*